Qurbaan

A Poet's Liberation

Zaira Pirzada

Qurbaan

Published in the United States of America by Lucid House Publishing, LLC
www.LucidHousePublishing.com

©Copyright 2021 by Zaira Taranum Pirzada
This title is available in print and as an e-book via Lucid House Publishing, LLC.

Cover art: Annie Del-Hierro Jost
Cover design: Jan Sharrow
Back cover author's photo: Kristin Hoebermann
Print book interior and e-book design: Amit Dey

All rights reserved. First edition.

No part of this publication may be reproduced, stored in or introduced into a retrieval system or transmitted, in any form or by any means (electronic, mechanical, photocopying, recording or otherwise) without the prior written permission of both the copyright owners and the publisher. The scanning, uploading and distribution of this book via the Internet or via any other means without the publisher's permission is illegal and punishable by law. Please purchase only authorized print, electronic, or audio editions and do not participate in or encourage electronic piracy of copyrighted materials. Brief quotations in reviews of the book are the exception. Your support of the authors' rights is appreciated.

Library of Congress Cataloging-in-Publication Data
Name: Pirzada, Zaira Taranum, 1992-
Qurbaan/a poet's liberation/Zaira Pirzada
Description: First Edition./Marietta, Georgia: Lucid House Publishing, 2021
Identifiers: Library of Congress Control Number: 1950495175
ISBN: 978-1-950495-17-7 (paperback)
ISBN: 978-1-950495-18-4 (e-book)
Subjects: 1.) poetry/poems 2.) women writers 3.) nature 4.) feminism/feminist 5.) love poems 6.) American literature 7.) activist 8.) diversity 9.) South Asia/south asian 10.) India/Pakistan 11.) inspirational 12.) politics 13.) self-help/self-love

POE005060
POE024000
POE023000

Lucid House Publishing books are available for special promotions and bulk purchase discounts. For details, contact info@LucidHousePublishing.com

Artist: Abhik Mukherjee

1.

The Magnificent

I am. I am.
        I am:

The beginning of every end.
The evolution of revolutions in becoming.
I am matter borne from matter:
The universe in every breathe;
The ancestors of the soil;
The greatness of Mother Earth reproduced.

I am everlasting.
        I am,

forever breathing
in the lines that paint my face,
in the grays that grace my mane,
through the body to be debris
for the green that follows the light.
I am the word.
I am the stone against the monsoons,
consuming tides and crashing winds

Qurbaan

while the Earth tilted on its very own axis
bows to the Creators of the energy that is
within me.

I am. I am.

    I am

        The Magnificent.

2.

Lovesick

I watched
as the night's shadow
slowly consumed you.

I forgot the pale fire
flickering from a lovesick taper
wasting away after
it was too late.

I draw in your absence,
your face glowing still,
your folded cheek on my pillow,
your voice quivering with love's tenderness,
a sweet yearning; you still ease
this dreary, this dark,
this empty calm.

3.

Longing

Longing drew by twilight an illusion in my bed:
lost desires haunting me ever yet
always teasing and fleeting by day,
your painted hands curled onto my breast,
and steady breaths from which your lovely words
and false hopes were golden
moments of past memories.
Please stay.

4.

Long-Distance

If it were easy to part
would then Angels separate
soul from body?

I cower under layers of myself.

Or would I like monks threaded
only to their vessels,
find you beyond the breathless skies
if even just to sink in your shadow—
in darkness it burns all the same.

5.

When I'm Home

Speak to me in my mother tongue please,
I am your child too...
Just disowned by the oceans that separate us,
I am only an orphan of foreign lands.

Their history writes me into the backdrop,
a whim for their Asiatic fetish,
a jester in their money courts.

My history is dead at the ends,
uprooted from you.

Speak to me in my mother tongue please,
I am your blood too.

Nani painted in in amber red mehndi,
they thought me a savage.

Ama made art of spice,
they thought me a savage,

Zaira Pirzada

And when bombs caved buildings
of those faces like mine,
they fed me fists to mask my face
with the blood of a savage.

Speak to me in my mother tongue please,
I am no one if I am not you too.

6.

To Love a Bailaor

Neck kisses in a back alley Sevillana hostel
ornate in abandoned beers and cheap liquor,
we moved to the echoes of youth in ecstasy.

You sang onto my scorched skin:
when I die
I will ask you for but one commission
that your soul becomes my soul
your breath my very own.

I surrender to our summer whims,
lost in you.

Forever eternal under the Spanish sun.

7.

Why Not

Adorn yourselves freely,
We'll be food for the critters soon.
Small bites of our traumatic skin will
keeps the belly of Earth full.

The histories and hierarchies
of humanity
are futile to the future
of the dead,
all ash and dust in the end.

The last breath of man
is his alone.

His lasting vision does not see class,
sees not color,
but only his own small existence
closing in.

So why voice less when
the ground will mute us?

Qurbaan

SCREAM.
Humm.
Cackle.

Stomp the grounds,
roll the fields,
and make an orchestra of life.
For time prepares slowly,
the delicacy of our end.

8.

Naught To Be Coy

When did Fall rise with the colored winds?
We blushed like the turning leaves,
pedaling through Prospect Park into Winter
when The Earth turned over in my bed
and drowned the howling winds.

How easy it is to replace the very seasons
and color them with you.

If time were our plaything,
how we would draw the very ways to color
an amorous day.

My love, seeded in the seasons
would flower into days to praise
every line, hundreds to touch
the darker parts of you,
and eternity to marvel
every forgotten mark.

Qurbaan

But the petals brown still.
Time overcomes the vast ideal before us,
where the hopeful lines of ageless love
we drew into the sand
fly, nestling into the lines on your face.
She gives us no final grave to embrace.

So in this very time,
    --youth in fire that browns your skin
        in the Caribbean waters--
let us tangle like birds of creation.

Strength and sweetness of naivety
together,
we'll fall prey to time that
makes the very Sun chase us still.

9.

Immigrant History

Our disposition,
              our brown bodies,
our blood,
              our people

soaked and matured the English soil.

The glory was meant for our roots alone,
    but we were no more than the same dirt
        to the Queen.

Within every fission
wrought onto our Pardes,
between the divides
they drew among us,
you can still hear us screaming.

10.

Janaan

Last night, I snuck into your garden
  planting roses.
I've no fear.
   How envious your other flowers are
    My Life of Spring,
these roses will live the seasons they die.
 They sneer, but
     I've lost count planting for you.

On my gravel-stamped knees,
  I dig,
in memoriam of Fall past,
  Winter's burdens,
Spring's and on rebirth:
   I think of you.

What am I? A crazed lover,
    I've lost count planting for you.

What I would draw for you full bloom:
   Gardens of roses!
What is a number?
    I've lost count planting for you.

11.

Last Text

I had stabbed the keyboard anxious, spited,
   with intent,

Every word was written,
   every phrase measured and said

—some I erased, and some I sent.

The others I chanced for a meeting,
  mulling over soured words:
    in showers and balconies high,
with ghosts that fell into distance's fire.

How blessed are my confessionals,
  with good heart
  honest and with stride,
    to the words of words do I owe
my peace
   lest the knife draw his blood with ire.

12.

To the Capital Masters:

I'm not good enough for the truth,
the same truth I stumbled upon
eavesdropping on your ways of being.
I appreciate your cheap thrills in degrees and art,
the many scapegoated years,
but I admit I'm resentful now,
ungrateful that the winners are sinners
and green all in between;
that my grit is your leisure,
my sorrows your antiques,
and these morsels of joy you offer
are charades to your own wealth.

13.

Purpose

Our inheritance from the Earth,
borrowed time is decaying.

Like evolutionary hogs,
we subsist on momentary gratification,
the taste of all good things
as ephemeral on our tongues as the sun
soaking the rose-cheeks of the young,
like hope renewed.

And so how do we
intend to eat the fruit
from the dying tree?

Do we follow the hoarded masses
to their half-day graves,
clocking out a step closer to death,
or the pandering few that have traded
passion for a nickel?

Qurbaan

Do we search endlessly like
those misfortunate wanderers for whom
the hourglass only descends into resent,
or find God in all of the small things?

14.

Pandemic Dreams

Last night you were running,
you'd only looked back twice at your people
choking on their own air.
Once upon my cough,
and another upon our shivered pleas.

15.

Let It Be Heard

While the blood of the son of the Son
of the Sun sizzles on stained cement:
I beg:
who taught us that black bodies
no longer feel pain?

That only one man can kneel,
and that is if upon the neck of the righteous.

That we must fear the very people
our state starves
that our silence is worth more
than their children.

He echoes from The Dark House,
a stout baseless thing to the mind,
putrid pontification of the colonial masses
leader of them:
those hateful preachers,
it is him.

Zaira Pirzada

It is them, always
but in this moment
it is him.

Let it be televised.
We will breathe together. We will feel together.
We will fight, and though they burn us,
we will rise, ashes to nurture a new soil on
this holy land of ours: the diverse,
together.

16.

Anxiety

This is an anxious cry—
like writhing frogs swarming in
guttural sounds
up to my neck,
         trapped.

It is to feel in my
burning eyes, heavy brimmed
like bruised clouds, inching so to not spill
at the behest of my nail-dented,
         clenched fists
all to tame the serpents body,
as it slithers, recoils, snaps
backwards and
         I crack just to speak.

17.

For the America that Made Me

I.

Somewhere on the rooftop through secret stairs of the Laundromat
where mom spent her last coin to dull the noses of the
white kids pondering my spiced closet,
I rapped to Biggie with my broken English.

A Commandment to failed systems that sustained
salsa on the streets, and Chinese below,
where I was little India, feeling the weight of being
more than America could help.

We: of alien lands, under Patriots, lived in the fabric,
indelible color painting necessary culture.
A reprisal to this bloodied Protestant utopia,
an unlikely outcome to the post-Native genocide.

How lucky these Stars and Stripes are.
The rockets red glare found us through railroads
stained in immigrant blood,
held steady by the bones of Tribes and slaves,
giving truth to the night,
that our flags are still here.

Qurbaan

II.

The (white) Ungrateful Shriveling Anxious.
This is the irony of the land of the free,
never liberated from the ruling gaze, and timidity
masked in exclusionary badges.

Imperialized neighborhoods, migrations to the outskirts,
shackles and cells suffocating our kin,
and redactions of our beings into the history
hidden between the textbook lines only
my brown eyes can see.

They love us so much, they watch.
They hate us so much, they hide.

The ugly truth is in their chaos,
a masquerading identity following roots
meeting lands to nowhere.
While our truth lives on our skin, and
sings from our tongues.
Jealously finds its reflection in
the America that made me.

18.

A Calling

Oh Protestant America
you're standing...
pouring sweat!

Your Supremes seem anxious,
they shiver with dread.

Is it because we are still alive?

Did you not expect the ghost shackles
to ring for justice?

The trails of tears and destruction you wrought
to guide future generations to right your wrongs?

The blood of this land, to be prepared
to rewrite your history?

The sins of of your New World
stain "equal" laws, and still fail
at every weak attempt to lament.

Qurbaan

The eyes of the oppressed are opened.
The voices of the oppressed are loud.
The bodies of the oppressed are ready
with peace, with power, with patience,
with justice, an action for us, all talk for you.

I fear for you, dear Old Protestant America.
We must all lie in the bed we make.
Welcome to your new history.

19.

To Prithvi Mata: The Vast One

The civilized will abort your womb,
pure barren.

Solemn songs will chant,
dying shrieks will rage through burning forests.
They will catch light to grow darkness
in the same shadows that your children starve.

I saw it on the news,
lifeless mature bodies holding their
dead on blast.

I found it in the oceans
where choked swimmers floated up
with their necks wrapped tight and bellies
full of waste, all plastic.

And under the light fixtures,
a man's joystick became a town's destruction.
Hands up for the drones.

Qurbaan

A silent death awaits your children,
in the name of wars for "peace",
they will abort you: The World's Womb,
conceive of you pure barren.

20.

Trafficking

What beautiful beasts those are:
dancing in chains.

The real monsters are the ones that throw paper.
Unearth monsters,
cogs in a wheel driven
for the lust of industry.

Have you met the ones in chains?
They are only free in their dancing.

21.

In the Last of Fall

I wanted to be the soul of the foliage
creeping up aged rocks,
nestled and tumbled into mountains across
which nature's wings climb,
then plunge
deep descents into the forest canopies
melting reds, oranges, greens and brows,
nature's blush to the chills winter winds crave,
when caressing her branches,
yet I am human.

A soul residing in nature's robbed glories,
burnt and bents woods, crutched
upon synthetic alloys: unusual comforts.
A foreigner in foreign lands.

I am unfamiliar work, laboratory Earth.
Make me the vines, the rings carrying age,
the confused nests and planted seeds;
a release from my humanity.

22.

I have never seen a poplar tree

but Black bodies are hanging in 2020,
so strangely normal to white faces
when black bodies sway on branches
there's blood on the leaves.

In Santa Rosa, a biracial baby boy saw his flag
clutched in the hands of a hanged toy monkey
whose neck was held tight by a noose
For all fun and games say Police,
with the toys and the free.

23.

The Pyre

I gave myself to the pyre of Love.
In the name of the highest infliction
my ashes run dry, though
embers still give to the wind
for all parting gives power to death.

To se lagi lagan.
I am attached to you.
Aisi lagi lagan.
Such an attachment occurred.
Khawaja ke liye.
For God.
Piya ke liye.
For my love.

24.

The Same

Every time feels like melting time,
    midday at every hour,
midnight only when I'm consumed.
    It's the crow that wakes me in a song for the living dead.

25.

Only Fans, Please

Watch as I overdraft on my shortcomings.
My insecurities find the most frivolous ways to spend
on mink coats of accolades.
Projections luster like fools gold while I blister dancing
to the same standard my world plays:
you must love me for me to love me.

I'll nip here, tuck there: table manners.
For breakfast plump lips, for dinner a big ol' peach
and let the babies watch as they suck teat
saline quenched while I suck fat from the unwanted ends.
Nothing wrong with a real lady,
the world will love me.

Break me to build me
"We can do anything, right Barbie?!"
Dress me in your mockeries.
Sex me to play me, and my soul you say?
Memorized lines since the media stole me:
You must love me for me to love me.

26.

The Court Jester

I have merely written revenge on ice
by dancing countless charades at your behest.
Under the Southern sun
no one knows the timeless cycles buried below Mason-Dixon willows like us,
where seconds were counted to a metronome of slapping heels,
silent arguments against Savannah gravel.

In the Pink House, the underbelly of a fish soaked in
sap stabbed and poured from trees
golden and striated into knifed diamonds,
easy to pick,
easy to nourish in death--but the peaches!

Oh the peaches colored in Summer dawn, haloed in orbiting flies
vulture-ing rotting flesh,
dented skin, but the fish.
The fish glistened alive in its grimace.
A happy stillness upon a couture plate.

Darling, do you remember the South?
Where I wanted to hang listless,

Qurbaan

pouring blood into cherries dripping from Tennessean trees,
curl into Hollywood cemetery with the Confederates fighting for a lost war,
in love with you.
I was the fish. I was the flesh.
The color of cherries. The tomb towering.
The Court Jester.

27.

Elementary Math

Do unto others, as you would
But humanity forgets.

One.

A body for a gun,
trigger slapping young babies brains out of
guilt turning the trigger onto himself.

Two.

Little Boy. Fat Boy. Clever hunger.
Charring and melting the wailing
bodies, shrieking in the future of nuclear detente.

Three.

Sides to every story.
The victor, the loser. The truth.
Armies spraying chlorine into the trenches of the young,

Qurbaan

swimming in the decay of blood pools.
Flying shadows peeling cement from the foundation,
wrapping broken bones, crunching under impact.

Four.

Man's blood soaks soil rich.
Species fall prey to sentient gluttony.
Empathy fatigue settles in.

Five.

This is how the Earth burns.

28.

Marks

I was thirteen running cocoa butter along my skin
patterned like ripped tights,
except you couldn't throw this pair out,
not the hips, not even the ass.

From the cement cracks of Brooklyn
I watch even the most feeble flowers bloom
In the sinuous paths of rivers,
I hear gold flows
every rip, every crack exposes a truth
yet I abhorred my body like marble shamed,
carved and imperfect from which I thought
my womanhood was to blame.

So many voices whispered my difference,
mocked my canvas, stretched thin to the curves
Imagine my surprise when they asked the surgeon for my body!

The secret is written in between the lines,
poetry paints my every crevice
in heavens flowing streams,

Qurbaan

blessings unsought from a lifeless scalpel
I was in fact gifted.
I am the entire woman
you could never buy.

29.

Quarantine

There in the bathroom is the same toothpaste,
running out, the same brush, always wet
and there in the kitchen the coffee machine
whirrs like clockwork, at the same time, same motion,
with the same coffee, for the same stained cup:
Where did this chip come from?

The only real change is felt in the numbers
as the calendar shifts, the scale weighs heavier
and the death toll rises so the revenue crumbles
for small business owners boarding doors in preparation
for the long-awaited riots
unheard in the silence of normality
when we saw the weather shift and heard the chorus of the world,
loud and deafening
enough to drown the shouts of those
choking in oceans to escape torrid lands
much to the same note of those muffled cries in cages
and trafficking-friendly deserts to the border of faux-freedom
who all saw time change.

Thus the sameness is itself a revolution for the blind,
the repetitive sound of having enough.

30.

Home-Bound

The map to which I pin home lives in the mehndi,
blood-stained on my Nani's feet.
I remember. Caked and coated.
Hyderabadi baked.

I imagine the smell of damp Earth resting
above the frozen memories of my motherlands.

My Motherlands.

Where the sun beats down on my bruised shoulders,
on the lacrosse fields where India's sweet oppression in
Fair and Lovely could not touch My India's Brown Skin.
Painting on me: New York.
You know I love my brown skin.
Still so far from home, far from who I am meant to be.

Rather, who my people tell me I am meant to be
as I live in fear of stains in white,
chalk over the color of my Earth,
brown and gay, always rebuked.

Zaira Pirzada

My feet sink into the gardens of Persian rugs in the States.
I imagine home in the various tongues of my family,
formed in the words of male oppression, modesty, and light.
I keep quiet, *besharaam* sipping my chai.
Sipping my chai.

In the depths of my mind, I am home again.
The tales of sordid Pakistan.
Unlike the Pakistan I see.
The outskirts of India,
Unlike the India I remember.

Trauma lives in the burnt bones of my lineage
drawing their
graves from India,
or so say the oral traditions,
all I know.

                        This I have inherited.
I have wrung into my Sari.
I have painted onto my skin.
I have sung into Sufi music.
I have carved into poetry,
and my wrists bare thin.

I have cooked whirlwinds of spices

Qurbaan

cracking to the hymns of God is one (and we are all the same).
And remained lost throughout my childhood in the states.
No rickshaw.
No sleepy dog reposed on the broken bricks of the Old City,
gazing into the prayer call.

Mind you, God loves all.
But not dogs.
Not pigs.
Not hooves.
Not Muslims in India.
Not all Muslims in Pakistan.
Not even Muslims in America.

The American God thirsts for Protestants.
The American God only cums to Christianity.
He only likes Bollywood.
He just suddenly started to like Gays.

                So I guess I pass.

Bollywood is my childhood,
where payal filled the house as I jumped one sofa to another,
as lava covered the floors.

I will love it.
I will hate it.
I will cry it sour-sweet sop into the shoulders of a lost soul.
Lost like me in this sweet, sweet oppressive world.

Zaira Pirzada

To which I danced along to the tune of the
high Brahman rich mocking the poor,
mocking the dark,
mocking the truth.

That this is all inconsequential for the Indo-Paki
breeding anger towards White People,
wearing bindis and taking pictures of poor people,
lusting my culture,
from which even I have been uprooted from,
torn within,
only to realize that if I go back
I will actively benefit from the cyclical oppression
of poor people, as a elite house guest
in my *Pardes*.

Home.
Some home.
Wherever home is.

Where it is, I will feel my sweaty kurta,
Cinched to my waist.
Big hips on display for the
shareef girl.
The good girl.
Never asked, "When will you get married?" girl.

Somewhere along the lines of a billion people.
I will be drunk on confusion,

Qurbaan

walking nowhere among the buffalos on the street,
dreaming sweet words.

And my grandmother's face,
un-pruned before death that called her too soon
yells for me to come pray.

I will recall watching bright fireworks on
Eid or Christmas, July 4th or whatever,
and my identity fades into the dark,
into the dark of my dark skin,
my darthi. My land. My freedom.

> They are happy,
> my people.
> I think,
> looking over the rains on NYC sidewalks.

About the Author

Zaira Pirzada is a multi-lingual poet, an artist, a technologist, and an academic. Her art is inspired by her wide range of professional roles and the double-conscious experience of being a Indian-Pakistani-American woman. A principal advisor at one of the world's leading information technology research and advisory companies and a board member of Women at Gartner, Zaira holds an M.A. in International Affairs focused on security, intelligence, and crisis communications. She is in the midst of furthering her education by pursuing an M.S. in Engineering in Data Science and Security Informatics from Johns Hopkins University. Zaira has worked at leading think tanks and appeared in international media for her expertise in intelligence gathering. Zaira, who won Miss Pakistan USA 2018, is also a Meisner-trained actress from the William Esper Studio and counts acting and spoken word among her greatest passions.

www.ingramcontent.com/pod-product-compliance
Lightning Source LLC
Chambersburg PA
CBHW062031120526
44592CB00037B/2201